TERRY ROWE'S
MOODS OF LOVE

TERRY ROWE'S MOODS OF LOVE

Lester and Orpen Limited

Also by Terry Rowe
To you with love
You and I, and Love
The Warmth of Christmas

Copyright © 1976 by Terry Rowe. All rights reserved. No part of this book may be reproduced in any manner whatsoever without permission in writing from the publisher, Lester and Orpen Limited, 42 Charles St. E., Toronto, Ontario M4Y 1T4.

Cataloguing in Publication Data

Rowe, Terry, 1936-
   Terry Rowe's Moods of love

Poems.
ISBN 0-919630-74-X

I. Title. II. Title: Moods of love.

PS8585.084T47   C811'.5'4   C76-017154-8
PR9199.3.R69T47

Printed in Canada

CONTENTS

Rainy Days/1
Trust/2
Energies/3
Mirror/4
Fair Game/5
Little Boys Don't Cry/6
Winter Winds in July/8
Truth/9
Reminders/10
Old-New/12
Souvenir/13
Easter Rabbit/15
France 1954/Toronto 1976/16
Games/18
Content/20
Memories in the Snow/21
How?/25
Help When Needed/26
Muse/29
Heartbreak Trail/30
Marriage vs. Divorce/31
Mistake/32
Fading Fads/33
Telephone Call/34
Fantasy/36
Perfection/37
An Old Man's Wisdom/38
Dali/42
How I Love You/43
An Inviting Smile/44
Fences/46
Children's Games/47
New Old Values/48
Knowing You/50

Memories/51
Thank You/53
Why?/54
Goodwill/55
Love and Like/56
Hearts and Arrows/57
Sensitive/60
Wish/62
Hurt/63
Roles/64
Return/66
Different/67
Are You Happy?/68
Shock/71
Horoscopes and Other Things/72
You'll Know/74
Remember to Ask/76
A Dream/78
Prayer/79
Loveless Life/81
Skating Shadows/82
To Mother . . . With Thanks/85
It's Time/90
Only Then/93
The Doors Are No Longer Open/94
Green Grass/96
I am Near/97
A Boy's Dream/98
Love's Hope/100

As always, for Joy

RAINY DAYS

*Did you ever
watch raindrops
through tear filled
eyes?
I have.*

        *Looking through
        windows streaked with rain,
        thinking of you
        and what might
        have been
        if you had
        been yourself
        instead of trying
        to be
        what you thought
        I wanted you to be.*

TRUST

*Sometimes
when I'm with you
I find
the thoughts
but the words
won't come.*

*Perhaps
the more
we get to know
each other,
the easier
it will be
to talk.*

*I hope you have
the patience
to wait
until I learn
to trust you.*

ENERGIES

We've walked along empty beaches,
our arms wrapping
each other in love.
We've sung and danced
to tunes
created by
flickering stars,
under the new moon
a warm friendly fire
now crackles,
and sparks fly
soaring with our thoughts
to the heavens.

As we love,
our souls stir
and we are closer together.

MIRROR

*People ask me
how to go about
loving others.
My answer is
you've
got to start with
yourself.
If you look
in the mirror and
don't like
what you see,
just remember
it's
not the mirror.*

FAIR GAME

A reporter
once told me
that
sure, she knew
what I was talking
about.
After all,
she had a genius I.Q.
To prove her point
she wanted me
to hold a rose
between my teeth
for the photographer.
I understood
her point
and refused.

LITTLE BOYS DON'T CRY

*I remember
as a little boy,
three or so I guess,
I fell and scraped
my knee
on the sidewalk.
It started to bleed
and really hurt,
and with pain
tears started to flow.
I remember
some adult standing
above me
(people are so big
when you're three)
pointing a pistol finger
at my heart
and my head was supposed
to understand
that big boys don't cry.*

*Well,
I wasn't a big boy
and it didn't matter to me.
My knee hurt
so I cried.
Today the pain might
be of a different kind
and it still doesn't matter.
I'll cry,
I'm not ashamed to admit
that I'm
human.*

WINTER WINDS IN JULY

*Do you know
what it's like
to love
and know
your love
isn't returned?
It's like
trying to run backwards
with your eyes closed;
it's like walking in winter's cold
on the fourth of July
and pretending your tears
are caused by chilling winds.*

TRUTH

*The beautiful
thing about
truth is
that it lasts
forever.*

        *The sad thing
        about truth is
        how infrequently
        we recognize it.*

REMINDERS

*I don't blame you
for teasing me.
You must think I'm
a junk collector.
I can't seem to
part with
old sweaters,
socks with holes,
part-pairs of cufflinks,
and memories.*

*All of those
are very dear
to me,
as is the time
and place we first met.
Or that special
song we used to
share,
our favorite restaurant
and the secret words
that had
meaning
only for us.*

*Old songs
and sweaters
and socks and
stuff,
all memories of our love
together.*

OLD-NEW

*I remember
an old iron bike
with folded
cardboard
and wooden clothespins
attached to the wheels.
The
exhaust
was the dust
of the
dirt road
as we sped
towards tomorrow.*

SOUVENIR

*I miss those knowing glances
you used to smile my way,
and the gentle pressure
of your hands
as your fingertips sent
chills up my spine.
I miss the ripple of
muscle as your hips
welcomed
my fingertips sneaking into
your back pocket
trying to come
closer.*

*I miss those walks,
the little girl giggles
you exploded with
once in a while.
I miss those days
of sunshine and showers
but the memory remains,
a souvenir
of love
shared.*

EASTER RABBIT

*As I stood in the cobblestone
market place
waiting for you,
I wondered if the
Easter Rabbit
in my arms would give
you a happy surprise,
and impatiently I worried
that the chocolate
melting in the hot sun
would ruin the chicken
and the basket of
marshmallow eggs.*

*It all seems so long ago now
but the picture book of my mind
tells me
of a love
that only father
and daughter can know.*

FRANCE 1954/TORONTO 1976

*Years ago
I sat in
my coldwater flat
looking out the
window at the gare
across the street.
Jambon sandwich,
munching workers
having lunch in
the middle of the
night while
most others
were asleep.
I'd listen to
Frank Sinatra
singing in the
wee small hours
of the morning,
and
his voice
provided
my only company.*

Now do you
understand
those
tears last night?
Seeing him live,
awakening
memories for
us to share.
And the voice
almost the same
as yesterday.

Only this time you were
with me.

GAMES

*Do you remember
the grown-up games
we children played?
Softball
with one bat,
one glove,
one ball
and a patch of
hard dirt joined
by uneven lines
of endless base running.*

                      *We pretended
                      we were baseball stars.*

*Some of us
still play games,
pretending to be
what we're not.*

> *The sad thing about
> the games we play
> is that
> we may think
> for a moment
> we've won.*

CONTENT

It's nice, just holding you,
the smell of your freshly
washed hair
awakening my senses.
The rapid beat of
your heart
seems to be a part
of me,
and I'm content.

MEMORIES IN THE SNOW

*I went for a long
walk in the snow tonight,
barely seeing
the mini mansions
separated by a bandaid
strip of concrete.
I recall other snowy
nights,
walking the streets
of a strange and
shadowed city,
friendless,
loneliness teetering
on the edge of despair,
wondering where I might
find a warm bed.*

*I shiver now as
I remember those dark
alleyways
echoing obscene whispers
that promised instant delight
for a fee.
Buses snarled,
and grey faces looked back
through frosted windows.
These were people going home
and none
as alone
as I.*

I thought.

*But I survived
to ride those same
buses in another town
and got to know how
people felt,
trapped, alone, insecure,
bill-laden mail boxes waiting
at home,
wishing they could afford
the white Caddy
passing outside.
I used to watch them
standing at the wicket
waiting for a turn
to buy my twenty-four hour
escape from the cold.
Then I'd sit through
two features three times,
and with proper planning
and luck of a newspaper
found the day before,
the program would change
the following day.
That's when I was thirteen
and had run away from home.*

*Yet I lived
and left town the next day
with a popcorn hangover
and I had the same
thought
as today in the snow,
keep searching,
this is your life,
you're writing your own
plot.*

HOW?

*How can
man
profess
to love God
whom he cannot see
and yet
consent to
the hanging
of his fellow man
whom
he can see?*

HELP WHEN NEEDED

*It was
an indian summer day
back in the forties.
Ploughing was finished
almost,
still had some
giant stones
left over from another age
to remove
so the wheat could grow.
Grandad and I
had just hitched up the team
when
our neighbor drove in
waving his hat
so we would know
it was important.
We walked back to the truck
and he asked for
help.*

*I don't recall
his exact need,
but I do remember
un-hitching the horses,
jumping into the back of the truck
and spending the day
working
at our neighbor's farm.*

*That night
as we milked the cows
and the coal oil lantern
flickered warm thoughts
throughout the barn,
grandad said,
when a man asks
for help
he needs it now,
not tomorrow.
So drop what you're doing,
no matter how important
you think it might be.
Then,
when you're in need,
you won't have to look
far.*

MUSE

*Inspiration
is the music
of the soul.
That's the
only poetry
I know.*

HEARTBREAK TRAIL

*Have you ever heard
of heartbreak trail?
It's that lonely road
where the only person
to talk to
is yourself.*

*You learn
after a while
that even you
don't fully understand
or trust
your memories.
Otherwise,
why do you
keep walking
over the same
ground?*

MARRIAGE VS. DIVORCE

*I understand
that some universities
are conducting courses
in creative divorce.
Wouldn't it be
a good idea
to also give courses
on what marriage is?*

> *The magic doesn't last,
> it's living and loving,
> giving
> and working together,
> and a conviction
> that two souls
> joined
> in body and mind
> are stronger
> and more fulfilled
> than one.*

MISTAKE

*I am
what I am today
because of
the many
mistakes
I made yesterday.
We all do—
though some of us
go around
thinking we never
make a mistake,
and that's
the worst mistake
of all.*

FADING FADS

*You don't see
many new gurus
around anymore.
They've more or less
disappeared
along with acid.
Fads are like that,
they come,
they go
and what's left
is a mild hangover
that slowly starts
to fade
when you know
that you
can be certain of
nothing
at all.*

TELEPHONE CALL

*It wasn't so long ago
that I stood in front
of a pay telephone
with a steel knot
in my stomach,
fearing
that you
might say
no thanks,
I'm busy.
Fear does that to you,
that unpleasant
insecure butterfly
feeling
when reason flys out
the window.*

*But the dime is
deposited.
(It used to be only a dime,
remember?)
After the third ring
the beginning of a sigh
starts to relieve
the anxious moments.
She's not home,
still hasn't said no,
and then a whisper
away from hanging up
the click of reality.
Good to hear your voice.
Sure I'd like to
go to a movie tonight.
And as I hung up,
ready to dance through the streets,
I realized
that there was nothing to fear.*

FANTASY

> I dreamed many dreams
> sitting in front of this
> empty fireplace,
> imagining our bodies
> decorating the red fur rug,
> the music from centuries ago
> softly playing
> as I wondered if my
> thoughts
> were the only reflections
> of which I could be sure.

I tried to imagine
where you were
and what you were thinking.
Now I'm glad
I found you again,
and we took the pain
to know each other,
to discover
the world of
you and I.

PERFECTION

*Perfection in others
must be seen
and recognized.*

But,

*that won't happen
until we
clearly see
the imperfection
in ourselves.*

AN OLD MAN'S WISDOM

*There have been many tales
of old men and boys,
but this
is of a different
kind,
because it's one
I know to be true.
The old man was an
Indian
who called himself
Chief.
And I have no reason
to doubt that
he probably was
once.*

*When we met
he was touring
with a carnival,
selling tickets
to his snake show.
I travelled with
him a while
and learned
from his example
that there wasn't
anything to fear,
I mean when I was fourteen
who ever thought of
wrapping a fifteen foot
python around your body?
Yet I did,
and wasn't afraid.*

*Then one day
he told me
it was time to move on.
You'll miss the music of
the carousel,
he said.
You'll miss the new
people in every town.
You'll think back in
years to come
and wonder
how you roamed this far.
You'll remember
how to spin the lasso
and make up Will Rogers'
stories.
You'll remember
that all you have
to do to know a horse
is to keep touching
him with your hands
so he realizes
where you are.
The bull whip I gave
you and taught
you to crack
won't take anymore
cigarettes
out of pretty ladies'
mouths,
but you'll remember
touching their faces
with whispers of air.*

*You may remember
my old eyes
and body filled with years
and the tears
we shed
when your pup was killed.*

*Now be on your way,
my work is done,
the carousel will keep
playing.
Your life
has just begun.*

DALI

*Sorry I'm late
again.
I got lost
standing in front of
Dali's Last Supper.
Awed by
each minute detail,
I was there
all of a sudden,
a part of that classical scene
from the mind
and soul
of a genius,
for us to enjoy.*

*Won't you join
me
sometime?*

HOW I LOVE YOU

*Instead of going out
with daytime friends,
I'd rather sit
at home and talk
with you.
I'd rather discuss Plato
with you
than meet a superstar.
I'd rather go
to church
with you
on Sunday morning
than play golf.
If what we
do together today
remains a joyful
memory tomorrow,
you won't need
to ask
how I love you,*

you'll know.

AN INVITING SMILE

Do you know what a newsie is?
I used to be one,
sandwiches,
soft drinks
and candy bars.
Rocking with the train
from car to car,
hoping to sell
all of the stock
so that the trunk
would be light when I
lifted it off
at the
last stop.

I used to flirt then too,
a smile,
once in a while
returned.
She'd wink
her thanks
for the sandwiches
and wave as I left.
I wondered
if I would ever
see her again
and then realized
I didn't know her
name,
                    where she was going,
                    whence she came.

FENCES

*Just as we
don't want to
see
barbed wire
around our land,
we shouldn't
build these
fences
between us;
have you ever
tried to climb
a barbed wire
fence?
No matter how
careful you are,
you're bound
to get scratched.*

*It's your choice,
but the answer
is simple,
love can't grow
with fences.*

CHILDREN'S GAMES

Loves me,
loves me not,
loves me,
loves me not.
Remember that
daisy flower game,
and buttercups
under the chin,
and rain, rain
go away
come again another day,
and practising
a new last name
and Mr. and Mrs.
instead
of Master and Miss.
And remember
that first kiss
and almost
passing out
from sheer happiness.
These feelings
can still be ours
if we stop long enough
to enjoy
life.

NEW OLD VALUES

We need new values
is a popular saying
these days.
Do we really?
I ask.
Perhaps all that's needed
is to remember
the values
of our grandparents
and their parents before them.
Maybe it's time we realized
that nothing changes,
except us.

I remember when we
said grace
before dinner in the restaurant
without being embarrassed.
I remember
when Thanksgiving meant
more than another long
week-end.
I remember Jesus loves me
this I know
and
now I lay me down to sleep.

                          I haven't heared much of that
                          lately,
                          it's the old values
                          that now seem
                          new.

KNOWING YOU

                I don't think you realize
                what I'm prepared
                to give
                to know you.

Sometimes
I don't even think
you care.
You may wonder
why I try,
why I persist
in spite of all
the obstacles
you use
to slow me down.

                It's because
                the more I know you,
                the more I know me;
                and the more you know me
                you'll know
                you.

MEMORIES

*I don't think
there's anything wrong
in remembering the past,
Orange Crush
in the old
dark bottles,
and how good
it tasted.
Remember licorice pipes,
five cent
ice cream cones
and singing
I've Got a Lovely
Bunch of Coconuts
on the way to school,
the first corn cob pipe,
how bitter it tasted
but you'd never let on.
Remember the first
home run you ever hit,
the stolen bases
and knots in your shoes
and broken laces.*

*Most of all
I'd rather remember
that first love,
that all-consuming crush
that made you blush
if anyone mentioned it.
It's all part of today —
without memories
there would be
no yesterday.*

THANK YOU

*As I was
writing you a little
note
today
to express my feelings,
three white roses
were delivered
to my door.
I wish women
would do that
more often,
not for me
but for those
they wish to thank.
I don't know where
to find you today,
Leslie,
but this note
is my way
of saying
I love you
too.*

WHY?

*How many times I've listened
to children
asking their parents,
why, why can't I?
How often I've heard
with sadness
the same response,
because I said so, that's why.
No wonder children
go to their rooms
with tears of frustration
stinging their eyes.
I wish parents would
understand that
any reason,
if clearly explained,
is all children are looking for.
Or
perhaps it's enough
to say
the answer is no
because
I love you,
that's why.*

GOODWILL

*I received a brochure
in the mail last
night from
an organization
that wanted me to
help spread the
word
of goodwill.
I might have agreed
but they used
the word
love
only once
and asked for money
six times.*

LOVE AND LIKE

>You asked me last night
>if I loved you.
>If I seemed surprised
>it was only because
>you didn't ask if
>I liked you.

It's really very
easy to love everyone.

>But liking someone
>is a much more difficult
>task.

HEARTS AND ARROWS

*As kids we learned
to draw hearts
with arrows through them.*

                                       *I could
never understand
that.*

*I used to say
to myself,
without a heart
we wouldn't live.
Without a heart
there would be
no love
no God
no life . . .*

*Without a heart
there would be
no you
or me.*

*So I stopped
drawing hearts
with arrows
through them
and annoyed the teachers.*

*Then one day
love's arrow found
its mark,
and I knew
the sweetness,
the pain
and lingering scar
were all necessary.*

*It's the arrow
that makes the heart
stronger.
Now, once in a while,
I draw a heart
and an arrow
and understand
its meaning.*

SENSITIVE

*You said the other night
that you thought
I was too
sensitive
for my own good.
I probably am,
but
would you rather
I didn't get upset
when you don't call
to say you'll be late?*

*Don't you understand
that the imagined steering wheel
pinned to your chest
in my mind is a real
possibility,
and I'm scared?
Are you afraid to call,
afraid that I won't
understand?
I'm sorry if you think
I'm too sensitive
but
call the next time,
please.*

WISH

> *If I could be*

whomever
I wanted
to be,
I would
be me.

> *And you?*

If you
had the choice,
would you want
to be
anyone
other than you?

HURT

*I've never slapped
anyone's face before.*

                *I didn't realize
                how much it hurt
                you
                and
                me.*

*I'll never
do that again.
There's simply
too much pain
already.*

ROLES

*I'm sick and tired
of roles,
of having someone
tell me that I'm stupid
if I enjoy
sewing and cooking
and am proud
of myself for doing these things
well.*

*We all deserve
the right to be —
in our own way.
Your resentment
proves that you
lost some of your
freedom,
and I don't blame you
for wanting it back,
but leave me alone.
I'm still free,
don't try to judge
me
by the rules of
your game.*

RETURN

*Did you see the
newspaper yesterday?
The big R
is on the way
back.
The big R
of the forties
and fifties
is filling
to-day's
airwaves.
Porno films
are less
popular,
the price of food
is obscene.
People are worried.
It's a time
when we need
each other
and the big R,
Romance,
is on the way back,
to help.*

DIFFERENT

*I tremble at times
because I can see
in your eyes
the hope
that maybe I will be
different
from the rest,
and what's more
I know
I could be.*

ARE YOU HAPPY?

Have you ever wondered
how many of us
are doing
what we really want
to do?

How many of us
enjoy our work?

How many of us
are working
only because
we have to?

*I know salesmen
who
wanted to be actors,
I know plumbers
who
planned on law,
I know a taxi driver
who
plays Beethoven
beautifully on a guitar.*

*If you're not
happy
maybe it's time
to stop
and think
and find
what more there could be
in life
for you.*

SHOCK

Shock to me
was the first time
I heard
a woman swear.

                        The next time
                        it was hearing a man
                        swear
                        at a woman

When I spoke that way
to you,
the sound of my voice
filled me
with shame.

HOROSCOPES AND OTHER THINGS

*I heard you talking
about horoscopes
last night.
It's very in today
to ask someone
you meet
for the first time
what sign they are.
But then again
there's a great deal
of interest lately
in the occult,
mystic orders,
secret societies,
fraternities that
flash diamond identifications
in the lapel.
Also,
reincarnation,
ghosts,
monsters from the deep,
the stars,
flying saucers from Venus
and the second coming.*

*I share an interest
in all of these,
but I think
that what we really
want to know
has yet to receive proof,*

*where is
Truth?*

YOU'LL KNOW

*Lately
when I turn
on an interview
program
that advertises
the topic love,
I'm disappointed.
They don't talk
about
love,
they talk
about
sex.*

*That's probably
the reason
so many marriages
haven't worked.
It seems
most of us
married
for the wrong reason.
We thought
love
meant sex.
It didn't take us long
to find out,
did it?*

REMEMBER TO ASK

*Once
as a small
and hungry boy,
I walked through
a strange apple orchard
and began looking
for the choicest apple
on the ground.
I found my apple
and was climbing the fence
when the owner
came to me
and said,
I've been watching you.
Why did you take
just one apple?
Because that's all
I could eat
before I got home,
I answered.
Don't you have
apples there?
No, ours are wormy
this year.
Come with me,
he said,
and sent me on my way
with as many apples
as I could carry
picked straight from the trees.*

*Grandad smiled
over the apple sauce
that night
but reminded me
that if I'd looked around,
I could have seen
the owner
and asked if it was all right
to have an apple
from the tree,
ask and you shall receive.
His words still echo
in my mind.*

A DREAM

*If we could
look over
the mountain of
trouble
the world is in,
we would see
the fountain of life
and drink
love in.*

PRAYER

*It seems to me
from the people I've
talked to,
that often prayers
are the result
of last minute
pleas
for help.*

                                      *And when some magic doesn't appear
to solve the everyday
problem,
the same people
that expected help
turn their backs
and say
God, what God?*

*Most of us
don't realize
that prayer
is a form of thanks,
for letting us know
that any problem
can be solved . . .*

*The answers
will always be found
within
one's self.*

LOVELESS LIFE

*There are those
who don't believe
in love.
What a lonely life
they lead.
How sad
to think of those
whose sole interest
is their own self.*

SKATING SHADOWS

*I watched
kids skating at city hall
the other day
and remembered
those yesterdays
when I walked for miles
to a frozen pond,
putting on skates
two sizes too large,
newspaper stuffed into toes.
We played hockey with sticks
warped, bandaged and
slivered.
The goalie's pads
were what was left
of last year's catalogue.
There was no time limit
in those days,
no music,
no cleaning of ice,
everyone skated
until they were exhausted.*

*Around four o'clock
someone always started
a fire,
and we'd leave the ice
to parents and little kids
to sit around
on old tree trunks
eagerly waiting
for someone to begin.
They always did,
and then
the minutes flew by
as we'd listen to
fantastic stories
about Teeder Kennedy,
of Wild Bill Ezenickie's
last fight.
The goaltender interrupted
the conversation
with stories that
made even Turk Broda blush.*

*Towards dusk
someone would mention
the Shadow
and the creaking door
behind which
some mysterious evil
lurked,
and we would haunt
the castles of our imagination.
Then,
did you hear
that noise in the bush?
Pandemonium as everyone
looked for his things
and ran home
till next week
at the same time,
providing the ice was still there.*

TO MOTHER... WITH THANKS

It's kind of nice that
we set aside one day each year
to remember with love
our mothers.
It would be nicer still
if we thought more often
of the many roles she plays
and of the days and nights
that could have been easier
for her
had we not been so selfish.

*How many times would we
have been late for school
if she hadn't kept insisting
that we get up?
How many toothaches did we
miss because she wouldn't
listen to an excuse
about something more important
than a regular visit
to the dentist?
And how many times would she
listen with that understanding smile
to our tales of woe
because we felt
we were so hard done by,
always with the same reply,
I know dear, but you'll
just have to try
a little harder next time.*

Yes, mothers everywhere
are pretty much the same.
Think of the vast knowledge
they have,
the trades learned
from a need to
give to others.
Mothers cook,
sew,
and mend lovesick hearts
with a knowing look
and a gentle, understanding
touch.
The budget
according to dad
sometimes really gets out of whack,
yet mom's always there with the
right answer
when algebra has caused
hours of torment and frustration.

*She's a student of medicine
and understands where the pain dwells
and how to help.
She's a doctor of the soul
and a lawyer of the heart.
Without textbook knowledge
she knows
right from wrong,
and how to bring us back together
when we drift apart.*

*I guess what we remember
the most
is that mothers
always seem to be
on our side
when we need that
feeling of hope.
She's there,
ready and able to cope
when we can't.
So, today,
to all mothers
everywhere
in every land,
this mother's son remembers
with thanks,
your love.*

IT'S TIME

*There comes
a point
when men stop
opening car doors,
send flowers only
on birthdays,
and give candy
in February.*

*Men should
realize that
women can see
through such thoughtlessness,
and have reason
to feel sad
and disappointed.
It's no wonder
they question
love.*

*When was
the last time
you sent
a dozen roses?*

                                      *When was
the last time
you said
I love you?*

*Don't you think
it's time
you
let your heart speak
again?*

ONLY THEN

*When you can see
love
in every flower
every tree
every drop of water
every animal
human or otherwise,
only then
will you be free.*

THE DOORS ARE NO LONGER OPEN

At one time
if you entered
a strange town
and all else failed,
you could always look
for a towering cross
and regardless of the denomination
the door would be
open.
I remember
falling asleep
in a wooden pew
very early
one Sunday morning
and being awakened
by singing birds
and sunlight
streaming in
through stained glass windows.
A gentle hand
stirred my shoulder
and a stranger turned friend
provided a welcome meal.
He didn't care
that I didn't know
where I was
or
that I might never be back
that way
again.

*I tried to find
that church
many times
over the past few years,
but each time
I was disappointed
by a locked door.*

GREEN GRASS

The green grass of spring
we take for granted,
it's beauty
isn't appreciated.
I'd forgotten it's sweet smell,
how soft it can be.
I'd forgotten
until yesterday,
when you and I,
in a lover's embrace,
lay on that knoll,
our heart's pounding,
our limbs locked,
eyes laughing at each other.
And then I remembered, as once again I discovered
our love,
the green grass
and the warm sunshine.

I AM NEAR

I hope that you know
I'm never really far away.
I'll share your toys
and try to tell you
adventure stories
about some of the lessons
I've learned,
some of the Captain Kidds I've known,
how David mastered Goliath,
about the Prodigal Son and
his welcome home.
I like to play catch,
and football,
I say my prayers just like you,
and when it comes to saying
I love you,
it's just as nice
to say
as it is
to hear.

A BOY'S DREAM

*I've watched you many times
over the years.*

*As a small boy
I stood
by the track
waving my engineer's hat,
hoping you would remember
me from yesterday
and wave back.
I used to hear
your shout
five minutes away
as you started to slow down
for that hidden bend.*

*Were you
wondering
how many summers
you'd spend
chasing air down the track?
And I wondered
what it would be like
to handle the throttle,
coaxing more speed,
shouting to the fireman,
feed her boy, feed her.
How my muscles ached
with imagined pain.
I shovelled
and thought of you
as part of my train.*

LOVE'S HOPE

*When the wind
blows through your
hair,
and the leaves
rustle beneath your
feet,
I breathe
the excitement
of autumn's air.
We hold each other
a little closer,
knowing
the trees will
soon be bare,
and hoping our
love
can stand
the winter storms
and we will be
together
to enjoy
another spring.*